The Crusades

THEN AND THERE SERIES
CREATED BY MARJORIE REEVES
GENERAL EDITOR: JOHN FINES

The Crusades

Second Edition

ANN WILLIAMS

Illustrated from contemporary sources

LONGMAN GROUP UK LIMITED,
*Longman House, Burnt Mill, Harlow,
Essex CM20 2JE, England
and Associated Companies throughout the world.*

Published in the United States of America by Longman Inc., New York.

First published 1975
Second edition 1988
Second impression 1990

*Produced by Longman Singapore Publishers Pte Ltd
Printed in Singapore*

ISBN 0 582 31096 2

Contents

Acknowledgements

We are grateful to the following for permission to reproduce photographs: Aerofilms Limited, page 11; Barnaby's Picture Library, page 6; BBC Hulton Picture Library, pages 25, 36; Bibliotheque Municipale, Boulogne-sur-Mer, pages 22, 28; Bibliotheque Nationale, Paris, pages 10, 15, 18, 19, 21, 49: Bibldarchiv der Österreichischen Wien, page 9; Bodleian Library, Oxford, page 47; British Library, London, pages 1, 8, 23 (photo: Weidenfeld & Nicolson), 33; Master & Fellows of Corpus Christi College, Cambridge (photo: Conway Library, Ccurtauld Institute of Art) pages 30 (photo: Weidenfeld & Nicolson), 41; A. F Kersting, pages 3, 32; Mansell Collection, page 17, 44; Musée d'Arras, page 34 (photo: Weidenfeld & Nicolson); National Monuments Record, page 51; Patrimonio Nacional, Madrid, page 12; Topkapi Museum, Istanbul, page 16.
Cover: Crusaders attacking Constantinople, from MS Laud Misc, 587 fol. 18, 14th century. Photo: Bodleian Library, Oxford.

To the reader

We often use the word 'crusade' today. We talk about crusades against poverty or crusades against famine. We call someone a crusader if he or she is very enthusiastic about a cause and wants to get something done about it.

This book will tell you about the first crusaders and why so many people in the Middle Ages went on crusade. In particular it will tell the story of the most famous English crusader, King Richard I and his encounters with the Muslim leader, Saladin, in the Third Crusade. There are maps for you to follow the crusaders' journeys. Most of the places mentioned on pages 4 to 25 will be found on the map on page 26.

Reference to money will be to pounds (£), shillings (s.) and pence (d.). Before decimalisation there were 20 shillings to the pound and 12 pence in each shilling. In order to compare this to money today, you could say that each shilling in 'old' money equals 5p today, so, for example, 5s.5d. = 27p. It is difficult to make these direct comparisons between 'old' money and money today because of devaluation and inflation.

Words printed in **thick black** are explained in the Glossary on page 55.

1 Jerusalem, the centre of the world

This picture is a map of the world with the Mediterranean Sea at the centre. The Romans gave the Mediterranean its name and it means 'the sea in the middle of the land'. People in the Middle Ages still thought the Mediterranean

Map of the world, drawn in the first half of the thirteenth century.

was the middle of the world and that the city of Jerusalem was right in the centre.

But this city which was so important for the Christians, because Jesus Christ had lived and died there, no longer belonged to Christians. It was now in the Muslim empire.

The Muslims

To understand how this happened we have to look back as far as the seventh century when a new religion started. A man called Muhammad was born in Mecca in the Arabian peninsula. He lived among people who still worshipped many **idols**. He began to teach them that there was only one God, Allah, and that Muhammad was his prophet, that is to say, he had been chosen to explain God to them. The teaching which Allah gave him was written down piece by piece, and later made into a book called the **Koran**. The religion which he founded was called Islam which means 'submission' in Arabic, that is submission to the will of God. The people who followed it were called **Muslims**, or people who have submitted – they had become totally obedient to God's will.

Friday is the holy day of the week for Muslims. People are called to prayer by the voice of the **muezzin** from the **minaret** or tower which is built into the **mosque**. Inside, the **Imam** who teaches Muslims the Koran, leads the prayers. Muslims have to say prayers five times a day and they are supposed to go on **pilgrimage** to Mecca once in their lifetime.

The tribes of the Arabian peninsula became followers of Islam and their warlike raids helped to spread the religion. In the hundred years after Muhammad's death the Muslim Arab empire spread right into Syria and Persia, and in the west as far as Egypt and North Africa and right into Spain.

The Muslims had many important trading cities. Merchants loaded their goods on camels and travelled together, in caravans, from one town to another, for safety on the road.

The chief mosque built by the Muslims in Jerusalem. It is called the Dome of the Rock.

In their great cities they used their wealth to build mosques and public buildings, like hospitals and schools, which **adorned** their cities. Their scholars were learned in science, medicine and philosophy. In these subjects Muslims were ahead of the Christians at the time of the Crusades.

At first the Muslims had been willing to let Christian pilgrims visit the holy places. They respected the Christians whom they called People of the Book, because they had a written **scripture** like their own. Thousands of travellers bravely made the difficult journey to Jerusalem to look at the places where Jesus had lived and taught. They knew these places from the Bible stories they had heard in their churches at home.

The Turks move west

By the tenth century the Muslim empire stretched as far as Persia and it was difficult to defend such wide frontiers.

Nomadic tribes of Turks from Central Asia wandered westwards looking for new pastures for their herds.

The men were fierce warriors who became converted to Islam. They used it as a battle cry to push their way into Asia Minor, right to the doorstep of the Christian empire called the Byzantine Empire. These Turks were called Seljuks after their ancestor Seljuk, and they established a kingdom in the area around Iconium. They carried out attacks against both the Arabs and the Byzantines from here.

Things to do

1. Find Jerusalem and Mecca on a map. When Muslims living in this country today turn towards Mecca, which way do they turn – east or west?
2. Think about the differences between the religions of Islam and Christianity. Make a list of these and then make a list of things they shared. Why do you think they did not get on together? Have a class discussion about this when you have made your lists.

2 The Mediterranean world

Look again at the ancient map on page 1, which shows the countries round the Mediterranean. You can see how the Mediterranean Sea links many people together. These were some of the people who took part in the crusades.

The Byzantine Empire

On the eastern borders of the Mediterrean spread the great Byzantine Empire with its capital at Constantinople. This city was built by the Roman emperor Constantine at a place called Byzantium, so you can see how the empire and the city got their names. Constantinople means 'Constantine's city' in Greek.

The emperors at Constantinople had a very ancient and rich court and were thought of as holy kings by their people. Visitors from outside the empire were always impressed by the emperor's royal appearance. One admirer said that his crown and his clothes, embroidered richly and studded with jewels, looked 'like a meadow covered in flowers'.

People in the Byzantine government and church spoke Greek. The eastern church was Christian, but it held some different beliefs from the Roman church in western Europe. Look at the picture of the Byzantine church on page 6. It was built in the sixth century.

The Pope in Rome

The Pope lived in Rome. He was the head of the whole Christian church in western Europe. It was he who summoned people to go on crusade. But the eastern

The church of Santa Sophia of Holy Wisdom in Constantinople, built between 532 and 537. The tall towers were added centuries later when the Muslim Turks had captured the city.

church and the Byzantine emperor did not accept the Pope as head.

In the north of Italy were the trading cities of Venice and Genoa. They lived by buying and selling. Both were looking for places in the eastern Mediterranean where they could trade. They were very willing to take the crusaders, their horses and their equipment to the Holy Land, but only for large sums of money.

Turks defeat the Byzantines

As the Turks got nearer and nearer to the eastern Mediterranean, which is called the **Levant**, the Byzantine emperors became increasingly alarmed. In 1071 the Turks finally met the Byzantine army at Manzikert and captured the Byzantine emperor. In 1076 the Turks took Jerusalem and now made it very difficult for Christian **pilgrims** to visit the holy places. Five years later a new emperor called Alexius Comnenus came to the Byzantine throne. He was so worried about the Turks that he decided to ask the Pope and the kings of western Europe for help against the **infidel**.

Things to do

1. In the word 'Mediterranean', which part means 'middle' and which part means 'earth'?
2. The daughter of emperor Alexius Comnenus, who was named Anna Comnena, wrote a history of her times. Your teacher might be able to get a copy of the translation of this in the Penguin Classics series from the library. See what Anna Comnena has to say about the appeal to the westerners.
3. Find out what Constantinople is called today.

3 The First Crusade

The Pope, Urban II, was very pleased at the emperor's request. He wanted to win back the holy city of Jerusalem and make the country safe for pilgrims. He also wanted to stop the Christians in the west from quarrelling among themselves. If he could give them a good cause, they might unite. He called together a council of bishops in 1095 and made a great speech calling people to the crusade.

Everyone present was so moved by his words that they jumped to their feet and shouted 'God wills it'. Then they began to cut crosses out of pieces of cloth. Fulcher of Chartres, a **chronicler** of the time, says it was a marvellous sight to see all the shining crosses made of silk, gold thread or other stuff that people cut out and sewed on their cloaks and tunics there and then at the Pope's order. Now you know why they were called crusaders, for the word 'crusade' comes from the Latin word for a cross which is *crux*.

Below: A crusader taking his vow to go on a crusade.

The crusaders march east

It was a long journey to the east and the crusaders suffered terrible hardships on the way. Even the Byzantines, who had invited them to come, were horrified at the bands of rough warriors who arrived in Constantinople. They wanted them to move on to Jerusalem as quickly as possible. Both the Turks whom they met on the way and the Arabs who held Antioch and Jerusalem, were unprepared for the crusading army. The cities could not hold out against the persistent **battering rams** of the westerners.

Above: This thirteenth-century drawing shows the siege of Jerusalem.

The capture of Jerusalem

Jerusalem fell to the crusaders on 19 July 1099 after a siege of six weeks. There was a horrible **massacre** of people which shocked the Christians in Europe when the news reached them. The trouble was that the crusaders had suffered so much on the journey that they had no pity left for their enemy when they met him.

Baldwin I receiving the crown of the kingdom of Jerusalem.

But now, at long last, they had done what they had come to do. Jerusalem and the strip of land on the coast were theirs. They then divided the lands they had won among themselves. They had many disputes about who should be king of Jerusalem. Finally Baldwin of Boulogne was chosen.

Edessa and Tripoli were made into small states with counts as their rulers and Antioch, an important city, had a prince. The crusaders tried to rule their lands in the same way as they had at home. So, for instance, the king of Jerusalem granted out four great fiefs, or blocks of land, to his most important subjects. They in their turn rewarded their soldiers with lands. In return all the landholders promised to fight when the ruler asked them. There were probably about 700 knights in the kingdom and between 4,000 and 5,000 foot soldiers.

The system had its drawbacks. The men did not want to come and fight too early in the year because they had their land to till and their crops to sow. They also wanted to be home again in time to gather in the harvest and pick the fruit. So two military orders were founded, the Templars and the Hospitallers. These men were 'monks' who made the usual vows to remain poor, not to marry and to obey their superior, but also trained themselves to fight against the Muslims, so they formed a permanent army. The Templars took their name because they lived in Jerusalem in the temple area. The Hospitallers were so called because, as well as fighting, they took care of the sick.

The crusaders settle down

Life was difficult for the crusaders, since the Muslims did not leave them in peace. The Muslims had the great advantage of fighting in lands they knew. They could also call up more men and more supplies and weapons quickly.

Remember the crusaders were never more than a small handful of men living in a foreign country. They only ever held the coastal plains and never controlled the important Muslim cities of Aleppo, Damascus or Homs. The people who cultivated their lands were the Greek or Arab peasants whose families had lived in the same places under many different rulers, Byzantine, Arab and **Frank** (the crusaders were called Franks in the east).

The crusaders were open to attack when they lived on their estates, so they built large castles. If raiders came, the crusaders could take all their people inside the castle for protection, with their animals and food, for a long period.

The only problem about these castles was that they needed a large number of men to look after them, so they were often left empty when the knights went off to battle. There were never enough crusaders in the Holy Land to make castles really work.

A modern aerial view of Krak des Chevaliers, 'the castle of the knights'. Find the Krak des Chevaliers on the map on page 39.

However, the crusaders and the Muslims were not fighting all the time. The Franks soon settled down in Syria and began to live in much the same way as the local people. Baldwin I is said to have worn eastern dress. This was probably because the long loose clothes were more comfortable in that climate than the crusaders' own thick woollen garments. The Franks began to take baths and to use soap. (The Muslim religion obliges its followers to wash frequently, and the dirtiness of the westerners was always something which horrified the Muslims.) The Franks also started putting glass in their windows and mosaics on their floors like those they saw in the east. They employed Syrian doctors, cooks, servants and labourers on their estates. Arab medicine was far better than western medicine in those days. The Arabs had inherited all the

A knight playing chess with an Arab.

medical skills of the ancient Greeks, whose books they translated into Arabic, and they added to this their own observations.

The Frankish nobles and the Muslim nobles liked doing the same things. They liked to go out hunting, often with hawks. They also liked to play games and the Muslims taught the Franks chess. It would have been surprising if crusaders and Arabs were not sometimes friendly to each other, but neither side forgot, when their leaders summoned them to fight, that they were engaged in a holy war.

Crusaders were still coming to the east. Excited by the capture of Jerusalem, a monk called Bernard of Clairvaux, preached a Second Crusade in 1145. The kings of France and Germany led a large army to Constantinople and then to Asia Minor. They were badly defeated at Iconium and Damascus, and returned home in sorrow. The most important reason for this defeat was that the Muslims were now preparing themselves properly to fight against the Christians.

Things to do

1. Write a diary entry of someone inside Jerusalem when the crusaders were besieging the city. How would they feel about the Christians?
2. Using the photo on page 11, draw a plan of the Krak des Chevaliers. Do you think this castle was a good place for the crusaders to defend themselves?
3. In what ways did the crusaders and the Muslims get along well together?

4 Saladin

So far we have looked at the Crusades very much as if we were crusaders. Let us now look at them from the other side and see what the Muslims felt about this invasion of Christians. We have seen how Muhammad inspired the Arabs with his new religion of Islam.

The Caliphs of Baghdad

The successors of Muhammad were called Caliphs or Deputies of the Prophet. They soon found that it was difficult to rule their large empire from Mecca so they moved their capital city from Mecca to Damascus and then again to Baghdad.

You will remember that all the stories like 'Ali Baba and the Forty Thieves' and 'Aladdin' in the *Arabian Nights' Entertainment*, were told night after night to amuse the Caliph of Baghdad. The Caliph mentioned in that book, Harun al-Rashid, really did exist. He reigned from AD 786 to 809. He wrote letters and sent gifts (including an elephant) to the western emperor, Charlemagne. They agreed that Christian pilgrims should be allowed to visit the holy places in Jerusalem safely. In the Muslim empire Christians were allowed to practise their religion if they paid a tax to the Caliph.

But all that was a long time before our story and we have seen why this peaceful arrangement broke down when the Turks invaded Arab lands. It was because the Arabs and Turks had been quarrelling and were therefore unprepared, that the crusaders did so well in the First Crusade.

Muslims began to feel that they must prepare to fight back against the Christians, but the Caliphs were very

A Muslim warrior riding a camel, from a thirteenth-century Arabic manuscript.

weak and they did nothing. So a Turk called Nuraddin built up a new Muslim state in Syria and Egypt. Just before he died in 1169, he appointed a young man called Saladin as his successor.

Saladin

You will see that Nuraddin's and Saladin's names look rather alike. Nur ad-Din means 'light of the faith' in Arabic and Salah ad-Din means 'honour of the faith'.

Saladin had been brought up in Baalbek, a town which is now in Lebanon. Like all Muslim boys he was taught the Koran and Arabic grammar and poetry. Some people who knew Saladin wrote about what he was like as a person. A doctor from Baghdad, Abd al-Latif, said:

I found him a great prince whose appearance inspired at once respect and love, who was approachable, deeply thoughtful, gracious and noble in his thoughts. All who came near him took him as their model. The

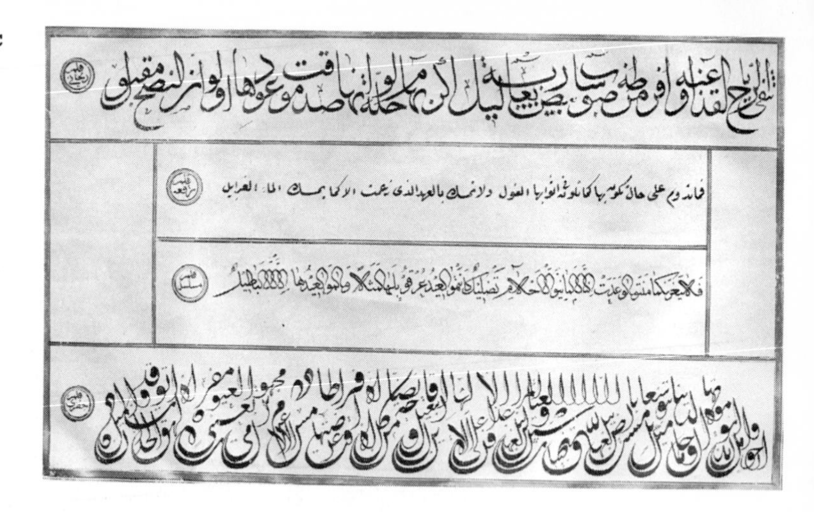

Examples of Arabic script. The second line says: 'We will make no treaties that do not hold water.'

first night I was with him I found him surrounded by a large assembly of learned men who were discussing various sciences. He listened with pleasure and took part in their conversation. He spoke of fortification, touched on some question of law, and his talk was full of clever ideas. He was then [1191–2] absorbed in strengthening the defences of Jerusalem and personally superintended the work, even carrying stones on his own shoulders, and everybody, rich and poor, followed his example. He was on horseback before dawn, supervising the work till twelve o'clock, and again from afternoon prayer till he returned by torchlight. Then he would spend a great part of the night in arranging the next day's labours.

His great friend, Baha ad-Din said: 'Our Sultan was very noble of heart, kindness shone in his face, he was very modest and beautifully good mannered'.

Certainly he was very much more generous to the people he conquered than his rival Richard. He never put his prisoners to death. But he was very anxious to turn the crusaders out of the Holy Land and for this he needed brave fighters.

We do not really know what Saladin looked like because Muslims thought it wrong to make pictures of the human body. This imaginary portrait was painted by the Persians in the twelfth century.

Saladin's army

The main part of Saladin's army was feudal, that is to say, men were given land and in return they supplied soldiers when the Sultan demanded them. The chief trouble with this arrangement was that the soldiers wanted to go home at the end of the summer to gather the harvest and they did not want to come back again until the crops were sown in the spring. This part of the army was divided into units, called tulbs, of from 70 to 200 men, each under an emir. In 1176 the size of Saladin's feudal army was about 6,000 men.

But he also had a number of other troops, or auxiliaries, to help the feudal army. He had to pay these men money to fight. First there were the Turkmens, that is the Turkish tribesmen. In 1179 Saladin 'sent to the Turkmens . . . thousands of Egyptian **dinars** to be distributed among . . . them as grants for their service as auxiliary troops,

Western view of Saladin's army.

and ordered that large quantities of flour should be made ready for the Turkmens and that they should be generously provided with necessities.' These men were very useful to Saladin in the Third Crusade and were really responsible for making Richard withdraw from Jerusalem.

Saladin also used Arabs and **Kurds**. Saladin was a Kurd himself. The **bedouin** Arabs were very good horsemen and enjoyed fighting greatly. Sometimes their warlike qualities were a nuisance to their employer. These were the men who, as you will find out, plundered Richard's army on the march south from Acre.

Saladin also needed foot soldiers, men to work the siege machines. A famous group of infantry was the black Sudanese unit which, as you will see, fought bravely at Arsuf.

Saladin defeats the crusaders

Saladin prevented the crusaders from marching into Egypt, and then prepared to invade the kingdom of Jerusalem. The crusaders were quarrelling among themselves because they could not agree who should be king. Finally they chose Guy of Lusignan and he marched out to meet

A fourteenth-century drawing of the Sultan's Guard.

Saladin at Hattin in the great summer heat of July 1187. The heavy armour of the crusaders was all wrong for hot weather and they suffered great discomfort. Saladin had a good army, but probably the crusaders had better weapons. Unfortunately for the crusaders, they did not choose a good position and wait for the Muslims to come. Instead they advanced towards them. The battle went on for several days and the crusaders were parched with thirst.

Saladin's sixteen-year-old son told the story of the end of the battle.

> It was my first set battle and I was at my father's side. When the King and the Franks had retired to the hill, his knights made a gallant charge, and drove the Muslims back upon my father. I watched him and saw his dismay. He changed colour, tugged at his beard, and rushed forward shouting 'Give the devils their answer'. So the Muslims fell upon the enemy, who retreated up the hill. When I saw the Franks flying and the Muslims pursuing, I cried in my glee, 'We

> have got them on the run'. But the Franks charged again and drove our men back once more to where my father was. Again he urged them forward, and they drove the enemy up the hill. Again I shouted 'We have routed them'. But father turned to me and said, 'Hold thy peace. We have not beaten them so long as that tent stands there'. At that instant the royal tent was overturned. Then the Sultan dismounted, and bowed down, right to the earth, giving thanks to God with tears of joy.

The kingdom of Jerusalem was broken by this battle and Saladin marched on to take Jerusalem itself. The city was sacred to the Muslims, as well as to the Christians and the Jews, because they believed that the Prophet Muhammad had gone up to heaven from there when he died.

Saladin recaptures Jerusalem

An Arab chronicler, Ibn al-Athir, describes what happened when Saladin and his army attacked Jerusalem.

> As they approached they saw on the walls a terrifying crowd of men and heard an uproar of voices coming from the people behind the walls that led them to guess the number of people who must be gathered there. For five days the Sultan rode round the city to decide on the best point for attack, for the city was more strongly defended than ever before. The only point at which to attack was on the north side. . . . [in September] Saladin moved his army to the north side, and on the same evening began to mount his **siege engines**. Next morning they were all ready and began their battery of the walls from which the Franks replied with other machines that they had constructed there. Then began the fiercest struggle imaginable; each side looked on the fight as an absolute religious **obligation**. There was no need for a superior authority to drive them on.

Bearded Muslims defending a city against the Christians. This picture was drawn in the thirteenth century.

The attack went on furiously for several days. The Muslims tried to undermine the walls, so the Franks became alarmed and decided to ask for safe conduct out of the city and to hand Jerusalem over to Saladin. At first Saladin refused. 'We shall deal with you,' he said, 'just as you dealt with the population of Jerusalem. You took it in 1099 with murder and enslavement and other such savageries.' But then he talked with his advisers who urged him to be kind and accept ransoms, that is, to take money, instead of killing them all.

The Sultan agreed to give the Franks promises of safety so long as each man, rich and poor alike, paid ten dinar, children of both sexes two dinar, and women five dinar. All who paid this sum within forty days should go free, and those who had not paid it at the end of the time should be sold as slaves. The city surrendered on Friday, 2 October 1187, a memorable day on which the Muslim flags were hoisted above the walls of Jerusalem. At every gate Saladin set officials to claim the ransom money from the people leaving the city.

Saladin then restored all the buildings which had been used as churches to be mosques again, and put copies of

This picture shows the Christian and the Muslim armies. The Christians had crosses on their shields, while the Muslims had a crescent – the symbol of Islam. (Today the Red Cross hospital workers are called the Red Crescent in Muslim countries.)

the Koran in them. Particularly important to the Muslims was the mosque al-Aqsa. All this had happened just before Richard I became King of England.

Things to do

1. Read one of the Arabian Nights stories to see what Muslims liked to hear.
2. Why do you think everyone praised Saladin? Was he really as good as he sounds?
3. Do you think the Christians or the Muslims behaved better at Jerusalem? Say why you think as you do.
4. Is there a mosque and a Christian church near you? What differences are there between the two buildings? Find out, if you do not know already. You could ask the Religious Studies teacher.

5 Richard I

This is an imaginary picture of Richard, painted long after his death.

Richard I, king of England, was the son of Henry II and his queen, Eleanor of Aquitaine. He spent much of his early manhood fighting to get possession of his mother's lands in France, and he often quarrelled with his father. In 1189 he finally became king of England, but he immediately decided to go on crusade. In fact, in his reign of ten years from 1189 to 1199, he only spent nine months in England. All the rest of the time he spent in the east or on the continent of Europe.

This is what one of the people who knew him wrote about him.

> He was a tall man, of good build, with hair of tawny yellow colour. His limbs were straight and **supple**, his arms rather on the long side, and for this reason they were better fitted than those of most people for drawing and using the sword. He also had long legs to match the rest of his body. His features looked like those of a king, and his manners and his bearing added greatly to his general appearance.

He enjoyed being a soldier and he seems to have been a good one. Even his rival Saladin admired him. Saladin became the bogeyman of western Europe. A European at the time painted a picture of him which gives him a green face and makes him appear very horrible and frightening.

The nickname 'lionheart' was probably given to Richard in his own lifetime. Certainly a number of chronicles and poems refer to his lion-like courage.

Why did Richard want to go on crusade? His father had made plans to go to the Holy Land, but he was too busy with his wars in France, and with governing England to carry them out. Finally Henry made peace with the French king Philip Augustus, but while they were talking the Archbishop of Tyre arrived from the east with news of Saladin's victories. Both kings resolved to go on crusade and agreed to set out together at Easter 1190. Henry issued a command in England for the 'Saladin Tithe', a tax to raise money for his expedition. They had just over a year to get ready, but they quarrelled again, and the plan was not revived until after Henry's death, when Richard became king.

Richard prepares for the crusade

Richard immediately began to collect men and money for his venture. He sold everything he could to get money. If people wanted to get out of going on crusade, Richard let them off in return for a large sum of money. He sold royal lands. 'All things were for sale with him, powers, lordships, earldoms, **sheriffdoms**, castles, towns, manors and so on', wrote one of the chroniclers.

Richard himself said, 'I would sell London if I could find a buyer for it.' Richard's army was made up of crusaders, both those who went with him and those already in the Holy Land. We do not know how large his army was.

Richard needed a fleet as well. So he had to collect sailors and ships. We still have some of the royal accounts for Richard's purchases. They were kept on a long roll of parchment called a Pipe Roll. This tells how much he paid some of his sailors. A whole year's pay for 790 captains and men (captains were paid twice as much as ordinary sailors) was just over £2,400. For another 174 captains and sailors Richard paid £529 5s. The Pipe Roll tells us that the king paid £257 15s. 8d. for three ships of Hampton and three ships of Shoreham. Walter the Boatswain's son sold a ship for £56 13s. 4d. Repairs to the king's own smack or 'eshekke' were £10, and the crew of sixty-one was paid £185 10s. 10d. for the year.

There were several sorts of ship. Busses, ships of two or three masts, were used for transport. One had room for forty horses and arms for their riders, as well as forty foot

Crusaders loading ships for the Holy Land, from a fourteenth-century manuscript. What are they taking on board?

soldiers, and a crew of a captain and fourteen sailors. Food for all these people for a year was also taken. Smacks were about half the size of the busses. In the Mediterranean there were galleys rowed by two banks of oarsmen. They were the battleships.

Richard and Philip Augustus go to Sicily

At last in June 1190 Richard met Philip Augustus for a final talk in France, and they were ready to go. They swore to share all the conquests they made and that whoever reached Sicily first should wait for the other.

Richard marched south to Lyons. Here the army ran into difficulties because the bridge over the Rhone broke when only a few men had crossed it. They had to build a bridge of boats to get the crusaders across the river. Then the two kings parted. Philip wanted to go to Genoa and then by sea to Sicily. He wanted the shortest possible crossing because he hated sea voyages. Richard went to Marseilles to meet the English fleet which was sailing round from England by the Bay of Biscay. But they ran into a terrible storm off Spain and so did not reach Marseilles in time for Richard. He waited for some days for them, and then, tired of waiting, he hired some other ships to get him to Sicily. The English fleet caught him up in Sicily.

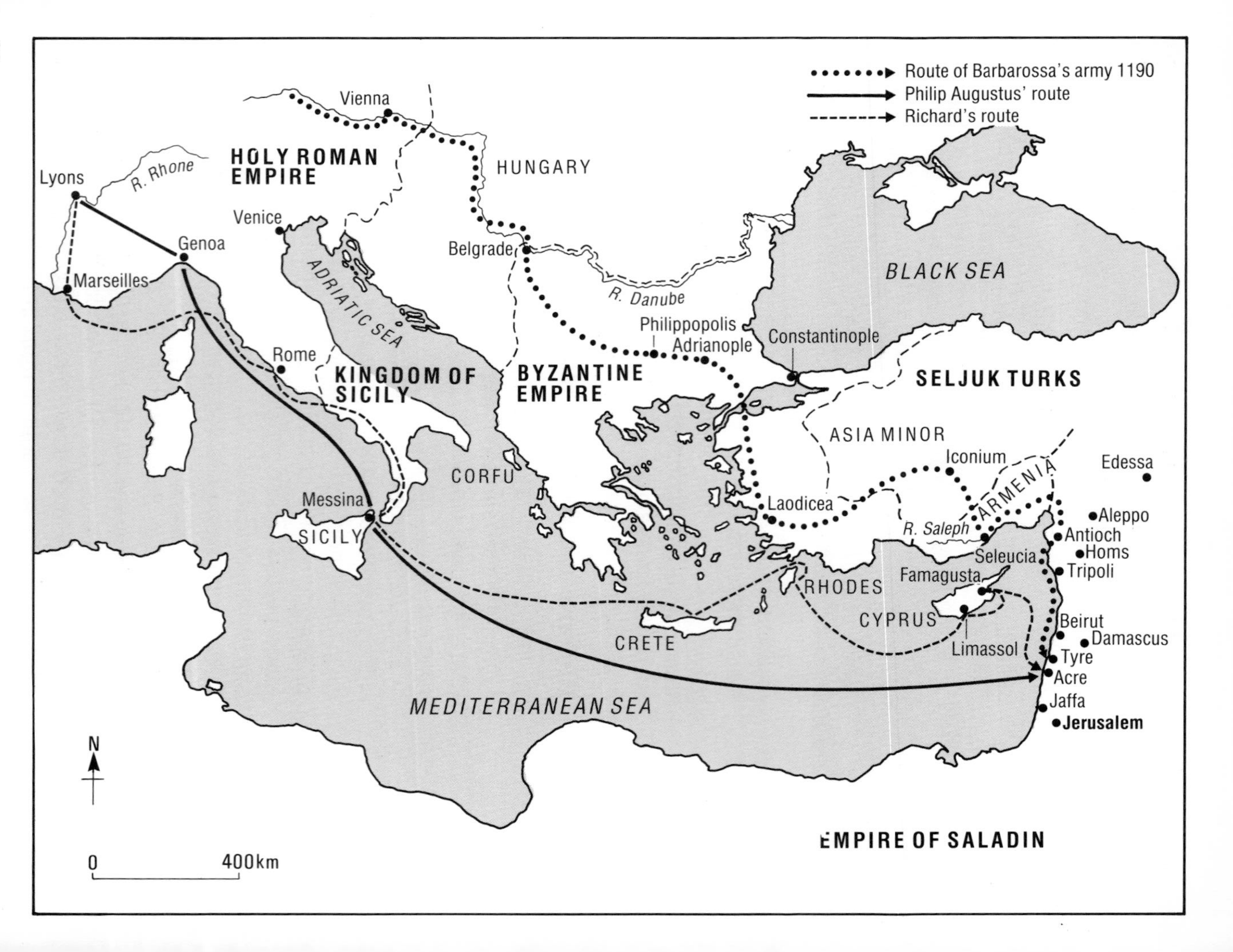
Route of Barbarossa's army 1190
Philip Augustus' route
Richard's route
Vienna
HOLY ROMAN EMPIRE
HUNGARY
Lyons
R. Rhone
Venice
Genoa
Belgrade
Marseilles
ADRIATIC SEA
R. Danube
BLACK SEA
Philippopolis
Adrianople
Constantinople
Rome
KINGDOM OF SICILY
BYZANTINE EMPIRE
SELJUK TURKS
ASIA MINOR
Iconium
Edessa
ARMENIA
CORFU
Messina
SICILY
Laodicea
R. Saleph
Aleppo
Antioch
Seleucia
Homs
Tripoli
Famagusta
RHODES
CYPRUS
Beirut
Damascus
Limassol
CRETE
Tyre
Acre
Jaffa
Jerusalem
MEDITERRANEAN SEA
N
EMPIRE OF SALADIN
0
400km

Richard's army went to Sicily because his sister Joan had married William, the king of Sicily, who had just died, so he hoped for some help for his crusade from the island. But the English were not welcomed in Messina. The new Sicilian king sent Joan back to her brother with only her bedclothes and her expenses. Richard decided to take Messina by force. A song from the time says:

Our king and his men have taken Messina
More quickly than a priest can say his matins.

King Philip Augustus had already arrived in the island and now the two kings began to quarrel. Richard's father had arranged that Richard should marry Philip's sister Alicia, but Richard was not at all enthusiastic. The Sicilian king Tancred caused as much trouble as he could between the two kings. The disagreement was patched up on this occasion, and Philip agreed to the breaking of the engagement before he sailed off to the Holy Land. Richard stayed on in Sicily to wait for the princess Berengaria of Navarre whom he himself wanted to marry.

Richard in Cyprus

Richard then sailed from Sicily just before Easter 1191. (Look at the map on page 26.) According to one writer there were 114 ships in the harbour, and 'as a hen leads her chickens out to feed, he [Richard] led his mighty fleet'. Because the ships were small the fighting men quickly got bored and therefore quarrelled with each other. Richard had to make fierce rules for the crusaders:

1. If anyone on board ship kills a fellow crusader he shall be tied to the dead man and thrown into the sea, or if he kills him on land he shall be buried with the body.
2. If anyone is proved by reliable witnesses to have drawn a knife, or wounded a man, he shall lose his fist. If he does not draw blood he shall be dipped three times in the sea.

Richard sailed by Crete to Rhodes and then on to Cyprus. This island was very valuable to anyone who wanted to fight in the Holy Land because it was rich in supplies of food and animals. Unfortunately for the crusaders, the Byzantine governor of the island, Isaac Comnenus, was no friend to the Franks.

Richard landed at Limassol and conquered the town. A few days later King Guy of Jerusalem came over to welcome him to the east. On 12 May Richard married Berengaria and she was crowned as his queen. We have no picture of Richard's wedding but below is a picture of a wedding of the same time.

Richard suggested a **truce** with Isaac and set out to meet

A thirteenth-century wedding from an illuminated manuscript.

the governor dressed in a tunic of rose-coloured cloth and a cloak, decorated with small half-moons of solid silver set in rows, mixed in with shining **orbs** like suns. He wore a scarlet cap and carried a sword with a golden hilt in a decorated **scabbard** edged in silver. He rode a splendid Spanish horse which had a red saddle studded with little golden and bright coloured stars, and at the back were two golden lion cubs, looking as if they were snarling at one another.

In spite of this splendour Isaac did not think much of Richard. He soon broke his agreement with him and fled to the hills. Richard and Guy then conquered the island, took Isaac's little daughter as a **hostage** and eventually caught the governor himself. Then, leaving troops in the island to ensure supplies of barley, wheat, sheep and cattle, Richard set sail again. The crusaders built castles in Cyprus as they did in the Holy Land.

Richard sails for the Holy Land

Richard sailed down the coast of the Holy Land, and just beyond Beirut, he saw a ship with three small masts. 'Only the ark of Noah was bigger,' said someone at the time. It turned out to be a Turkish ship which at once began the attack. This is how one of the chroniclers describes the great sea fight that followed:

> Our men plunged eagerly into the sea and getting under the enemy's ship, bound the helm with ropes so as to make the ship lean to one side. Others leapt on board but the Turks were ready and quickly killed them, pitching the dead bodies out to sea. Then more Christians came scrambling over the ship's side and hurling themselves on the Turks. So the fight went on, until the Turks forced our men back and forced them to leave the ship. So our galleymen began to row round the ship looking for a place to attack again. But the King, seeing the danger to his men, ordered his

A sea battle drawn in a fourteenth-century manuscript. The pots which the men are hurling contain 'Greek fire', a mixture which exploded when the containers broke.

> galleys to prick the enemy ship with their iron beaks [which were mounted at the front]. So the galleys drew back a space and then swept forward – with all the oarsmen rowing as hard as they could – to pierce the enemy's sides. In this way the ship was holed and began to sink, while the Turks leapt into the sea and were either drowned or captured.

The ship had been carrying men and reinforcements from Saladin's brother for the city of Acre, which was under attack.

Things to do

1. Why did Richard I and Philip Augustus, who both had plenty to do defending their kingdoms at home, decide to go on a crusade? Follow their routes on the map on page 26. What do you think the people of England thought about their king leaving them?
2. Look carefully at what Richard did on his way east. What did he do that was 'lionhearted'? Did he do anything that you would criticise? Discuss this in class.
3. Draw a picture map of what happened on Richard's journey to the Holy Land.
4. Make up what you think would be some good rules for crusaders.

6 The Third Crusade

When Richard reached land Philip Augustus was already there because he had gone straight from Sicily to Syria. Another western ruler, the Emperor Frederick Barbarossa, (his second name means 'redbeard') had promised to join them. He brought his army overland from Germany.

Frederick Barbarossa drowned

When he reached northern Syria he was drowned in the swift flowing river Saleph. A chronicler who wrote about his reign explained what happened.

> On June 10 the advance unit of the army camped on the plains of Seleucia. Up to this point the whole army . . . the rich and the poor, the sick and those who seemed healthy – had journeyed through the glare of the sun and the burning heat of summer along a very difficult road which led them across rocky cliffs which only birds and mountain goats normally reached. The Emperor, who had shared in all the dangers, wished both to cool down and to avoid climbing the mountain peak. So he attempted to swim across the very swift Seleph river. Wise though he was in other ways, the Emperor foolishly tried his strength against the current and the power of the river. Although everyone tried to stop him, he entered the water and plunged into a whirlpool. He who had often escaped great dangers, perished miserably.

The picture on page 32 shows the river with the castle of Seleucia on the hill above it. There was no bridge at the

A modern photograph of the castle of Seleucia.

time when the German army reached the place. Some of Frederick's knights continued their journey and joined the crusades, but some felt very discouraged and went home.

The siege of Acre

The first problem for the crusaders was to conquer the town of Acre. It was very important for both sides because it was a seaport, and both the crusaders and the Muslims could bring ships with men and supplies into its harbour. You will remember the Turkish ship sunk by Richard.

When Richard arrived the town was being held by Saladin's men. The crusaders spread themselves around the walls. They used everything they could think of to crack through the thick fortifications. They built towers and scaling ladders, and even spent the nights digging earth to fill in the moats of the town so that they could get closer to the walls.

In the Holy Land people had to rely on deep ditches round towns and castles, without water, because there was very little rainfall. But these dry moats could be just as much of a nuisance, as the defenders often put spiky stakes or large stones in them to make it as difficult as possible for the besiegers.

An eleventh-century plan of the town of Acre.

Another way to get into a castle or a fortified town was to put long ladders up against the walls to climb to the top. This was very tricky if you were carrying weapons, and the people inside the town could often knock down the ladders, or pick off the men coming up, one by one, with arrows. One of Richard's scaling ladders was called 'the cat' because after creeping up like a cat it grasped the wall and stuck fast to it.

Richard's arrival caused great joy in the Christian army. They blew trumpets and shouted welcomes as he came ashore. From his camp Richard and his men could see Saladin's tents and even his tame lions on the hillside. Saladin was trying to get food and weapons into the besieged city so the crusaders had two problems: to try to conquer Acre, and to stop Saladin helping the people inside the city before they stormed it.

Philip Augustus had a very good siege engine called 'the bad neighbour', while the Muslims inside the city had one called 'the bad relative'. Philip kept rebuilding his in order to attack the tower called 'the accursed tower'.

The crusaders also had slings with stones. One stone was so huge that it killed twelve men and Saladin himself asked to see it. The crusaders also used a machine with a framework made of woven sticks and covered with animal hides. The archers hid underneath it and shot off their arrows. This was called the 'circleia'. Richard sent his sappers, or miners, to make an underground passage beneath the tower at which his seige engines were firing. They filled up the hole with timbers which they set on fire.

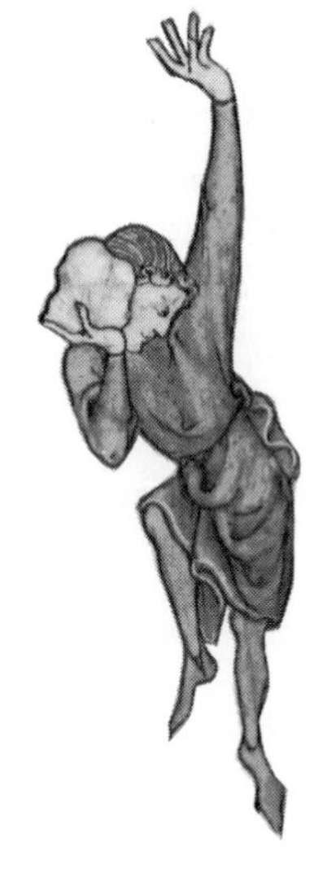

One of the men carrying a stone to get his gold, from a thirteenth-century manuscript.

Richard knew that all the soldiers were anxious to get as much plunder as they could, so he ordered men to go round the camp announcing that anyone who removed a stone from the wall next to the tower would receive two pieces of gold from the king. Later he promised three gold pieces and then four, so that however many stones anyone removed, he received a payment of four gold pieces for each. The young men swarmed to the wall. When the stones were taken out they would go on eagerly, greedy for praise as well as for payment. Even in the midst of the enemy's missiles they worked on bravely at tearing down the wall.

Acre captured by the crusaders

It was impossible for Saladin to get supplies into the besieged city so he sent a message to the men inside telling them to give in to Richard. The Muslims had to promise to hand over Acre with everything in it, weapons and ships. The Franks were to have 200,000 pieces of gold and 1,500 prisoners. They were also to have the True Cross on which Jesus was crucified, which the Muslims had captured earlier in the crusades. Saladin was deeply upset at these harsh terms. Richard behaved very cruelly and beheaded a large number of prisoners.

Richard and Philip Augustus were friends at this moment as the chronicler who wrote about Richard's journey said:

> When all the Turks had left the city, the Christians, on the orders of the two kings, opened the gates and freely entered the city, joyfully dancing and exulting at the tops of their voices. They glorified the Lord and gave thanks for God had showed his great mercy to them. The banners and many flags of the kings were up on top of the walls and towers. The city was equally divided by the kings. They also made an equal distribution of the supplies of arms and food between their armies. They drew lots for the most important and richest prisoners. The King of France had for his part the noble palace of the Templars with all its possessions. King Richard got the royal palace, to which he sent his queen with the children and their servants. Thus each of the kings peacefully secured his position. The army was housed throughout the city.

But Philip Augustus had had enough of crusading and decided to return home to France. Look at the picture on page 36 which shows him leaving the Holy Land. Richard was furious and asked the French king to promise that he would be faithful to their friendship and not stir up trouble in Richard's lands at home. Philip did take the oath, but he broke it as soon as he reached home.

Richard marches toward Jerusalem

Richard made more rules to keep the soldiers in order.

1. If anyone speaks ill of another he shall pay an ounce of silver.

A fourteenth-century drawing of Philip Augustus leaving the Holy Land. He has the 'fleur-de-lys' emblem of France on his shield and tunic.

2. If anyone is convicted of stealing he shall have his head shaved, then covered with boiling pitch and covered with feathers.

The ordinary soldiers were forbidden to gamble. Knights and Clerks were not to lose more than 20 **solidi** in twenty-four hours. If they did they were to pay 100 solidi to the crusade treasury. The kings could play whenever they liked.

So Richard was left alone in charge of the crusading army. His next plan was to march south towards Jerusalem which was the real object of the crusade. Many of the crusaders did not want to leave Acre because of the easy life they were enjoying there, but the king forced them on. His plan of campaign was to march along the coast so that he would have the support of his ships. He decided to go to Jaffa and Ascalon and make a base camp there, and then to strike inland to the Holy City. The route was a difficult one. There were eight rivers to cross and it was the hottest time of the year. Many of the crusaders, fainting from the heat, dropped dead and were buried where they fell. All along the road were wooded hills where Saladin's men could hide, ready to pounce on the marching crusaders.

One of the chroniclers describes how the Turks worried the marching army like flies:

> The Turks are not weighed down with armour like our men. They carry only a bow, a club with sharp teeth, a sword, a lance and a knife. When defeated they flee away on the swiftest horses, but when they see their pursuers slackening in the pursuit, they stop fleeing and return like a persistent fly which, though you drive if off, will return directly you stop your efforts. It is just like that with the Turk. When you stop trying to catch him, he returns to worry you.

The chronicler tells us how the Franks camped at night.

> Every evening, before men went to rest, a certain person cried out in the middle of the army: 'Help us, Holy Sepulchre!' Then the whole crowd would take up the cry, stretching out their hands to heaven and shedding many tears, praying to God for help. Every night creeping insects called tarantula spiders used to annoy our men with burning stings, although they did no harm in the daytime. But we found out that you could drive them away with a great noise so, whenever they came near, we began to make a frightful din and clatter, with shields, helmets, poles, jars, jugs, basins, pans, plates and anything else that was handy for making a noise.

The battle at Arsuf

Saladin decided he would try to force the crusaders to a pitched battle near Arsuf. He had a large army collected and he knew the crusaders were tired because of the march. Find Arsuf on the map on page 39.

On Saturday, 7 September 1191, the armies were facing one another. Richard arranged his men carefully. They were divided into five battalions. The Templars led the first rank, then the Bretons and the men of Anjou. King

Guy, with the men of Poitiers, was next, with the Normans and the English, who were carrying the royal banner, on their other side. Finally came the Hospitallers. The army was drawn up between Saladin and the sea.

On the other side Saladin was said to have a force of more than 20,000. Most frightening to the crusaders was a company of black Sudanese warriors who were very fine foot soldiers. The noise of drums, pipes, rattles and **cymbals** made the approach of the Muslim army fearful to hear and see.

This is how the chronicler describes the fighting.

> The third hour [9 a.m.] was now drawing on, when lo! a host of Turks swept rapidly down on our men, hurling darts and arrows, and making a terrible din with their confused cries. On horses swifter than eagles they thundered down on us, till the whirling dust blackened the air. Our little flock of people was hemmed in on every side and, like a flock of sheep in the jaws of the wolves, we could see nothing except the sky and our fierce enemies. The Turks kept up the shower of arrows and darts until the brightness of the sun itself grew dark, as in a storm of hail.

Bitter fighting went on all day until at last King Richard led a fierce attack which defeated and drove off the Muslim army.

Richard fails to capture Jerusalem

This battle was Richard's greatest success in the Holy Land, but he could not follow up his victory. He tried twice to march up and capture Jerusalem. The crusaders were longing for this, since they desired very greatly to see Jerusalem and go home. The chronicler describes how they got ready for the march.

> Each man carried his own food, so as to get the siege [of Jerusalem] finished soon. **Breast-plates** were scrubbed in case any rust should stain them: helmets

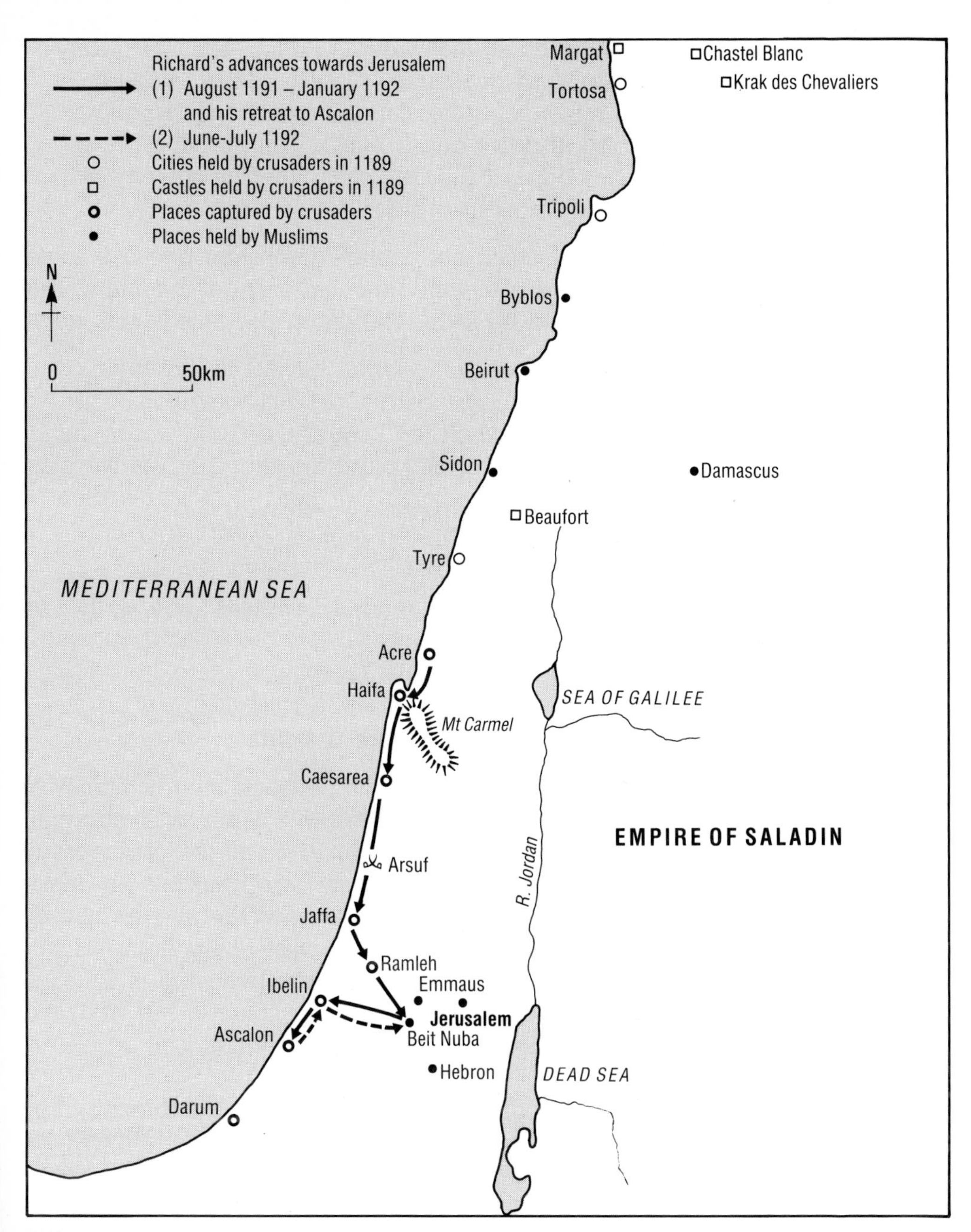

Richard advances towards Jerusalem.

were polished so that creeping damp should not dim their gleam; sword-blades were greased. When the herald announced the start, all men began to rejoice as a bird at dawn of day and to call out: 'We praise thee, O God, because we shall now see the city in which the Turks have dwelt for so long.'

But Richard could not capture Jerusalem because some of his allies deserted him. He could only get to a hill where Jerusalem could be seen. The chronicler tells us this story:

There came one of the king's knights to him crying out: 'Sire, sire, come here and I will show you Jerusalem!' But when the king heard these words, he threw his coat of arms before his eyes, and he wept as he called upon our Lord: 'Fair Lord God, I pray thee not to let me see thy Holy City, if so be I may not rescue it out of the hands of thy enemies.'

So King Richard and his crusaders turned back sadly and retreated to the coast.

Richard and Saladin make a truce

Neither Richard nor Saladin had enough men or money to conquer the whole land, though Saladin was stronger, because he did not have so far to go as the crusaders to get fresh supplies. Both kings were anxious to make peace. Saladin's army wanted to go home and he himself was not well. Richard wondered what Philip Augustus was up to and how his brother John was behaving in England in his absence and he wanted to go home to see what was happening there. So a truce for five years was agreed in September 1192.

The Christians did very well from the agreement. They were given all the towns on the coast as far south as Jaffa. Once again Christian pilgrims were free to visit Jerusalem. Richard and Saladin exchanged messages. There was even a suggestion that Richard's sister Joan should marry

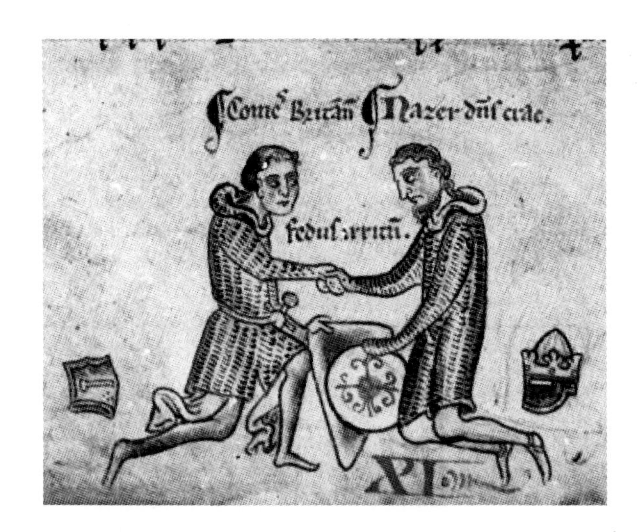

The truce between Richard and Saladin.

Saladin's brother, but in the end nothing came of the plan because she refused to marry a Muslim. Richard said he would be back again as soon as he had settled the troubles in his own kingdom. Saladin replied that he fought against no better king than Richard.

Things to do

1. Make yourself a crusader costume, with armour, helmet, sword and shield. You can use thick knotted squares, painted silver, for chain mail. Paint a lion or some other picture on your shield so that you can be recognised.
2. Think again about how the Christian kings behaved. How good were these crusaders and how bad? Make lists.
3. It must have been hard going on the road to Jerusalem, and a bitter disappointment when, in sight of the city, they had to turn back. Make up a song about the sadness of the crusaders when their crusade failed.
4. Write a letter from Lady Joan turning down the offer of marriage to Saladin's brother, El Adil.

7 What happened afterwards

Richard set sail from the Holy Land intending to go home the same way he had come, but he had news that Philip Augustus was stirring up trouble against him. He changed his plans and decided to sail up the Adriatic Sea and then go overland. Although he did not realise it, this was not a very good idea either. The new emperor of Germany, Henry, also disliked him and was jealous of his success in the Holy Land.

Richard's voyage was very rough. He ran into pirates and then into a bad storm. Fearing that the ship might sink he promised he would spend 100,000 **ducats** in building a church if he came safely ashore. He later kept his word by giving money to the cathedral in Ragusa when he landed. But his bad luck continued, for when he set sail again, another storm wrecked him near Venice.

Richard captured and imprisoned

When he began his journey overland the Duke of Austria, who was a subject of the emperor, had him imprisoned in a lonely castle at Durnstein. The emperor was very pleased and wrote to Philip Augustus that 'the foe of our Empire and disturber of your realm, the King of England', was safely in captivity.

When the nobles in England heard of Richard's fate they sent Bishop Savaric of Bath to talk to the emperor and to arrange a ransom for him.

Richard's song

There is a story told by a French **minstrel** about seventy years after this, that Blondel, the king's minstrel, travelled about with his lute singing at every castle to find where his master was imprisoned. The story says that when he came to the right castle Richard heard him and sang a song in reply. This story may, or may not, be true. No one knows for certain. But we do actually have a song that Richard wrote while he was in prison. Here it is in the old French the king and his court would have spoken. (The ordinary people in England spoke English.)

Je nus hons pris ne dira sa raison
adroitment, se dolantement non.
mes par confort puet il fere chancon,
moult ai amis, mes povre sont il don;
honte en avront, se por ma reancon
sui ces deus yvers pris.

Ce sevent bien mi homme ry mi baron,
Englois, Normant, Poitevin et Gascon,
que je n'Avoie si povre conpaignon,
cui je laissasse por avoir en prixon,
je nel di pas por nule retracon,
mes encor sui ge pris.

(No prisoner will ever state his case cleverly, he will put it in a sorrowful way. He can, however, write a song to comfort himself. I have many friends but their gifts are few in number. They will be shamed if I remain in captivity these two winters because my ransom is not paid.

My men and barons, from England, Normandy, Poitou and Gascony, know that if I had a poor companion, I would not leave him in prison, however humble he was, if it was just a question of money. I don't say this as a reproach, but I am still held a prisoner.)

Richard is ransomed and comes home

It was finally decided that Richard's ransom should be £100,000. The messengers from England went home and in less than six months were back with the money that the emperor wanted before Richard was released. Henry reluctantly let his important prisoner go.

Richard then continued his journey home after two years in prison. He was greeted very enthusiastically by the people, and the city of London was gaily decorated for his arrival. But he still had problems to face in England and in France. His last years were spent in fighting Philip Augustus.

Richard's death

Richard died in 1199 and was buried with his father and mother at Fontrevault. A poet called Gaucelon Faidit wrote a lament about the king's death. He wrote it in French poetry and this is an English translation.

> I must tell in song the greatest misfortune and sorrow that, alas, I have ever known and which, from now on, I shall always regret and lament . . . for the head and father of valour, the courageous and powerful king of the English, Richard, is dead. Alas! oh God! What a great loss and what pity! What a harsh word and how painful it is to hear it. The man who can endure this pain must, indeed, have a hard heart.

Below: The effigy of Richard I which is at Fontrevault in France.

Ah! Lord God! You who are merciful, true God, true man, and the true life, have mercy! Pardon him, for he has great need of your compassion. Do not consider his sins, but remember how he was going to serve you!

What happened to Saladin

After Saladin had signed the treaty with Richard he let his tired soldiers go home. He also made sure that the Christian pilgrims to Jerusalem were well treated and allowed to see everything they wanted to see. He entertained the Bishop of Salisbury and gave him many presents. His happiest hours were spent at his country house near Damascus playing with his children. But in February 1192 Saladin caught a chill while out riding and died of fever a few days later.

Things to do

1. If you are learning French, look carefully at the words of Richard's song on page 43. Pick out the words for song, friends, men, poor companion, prison. Remember that the spelling is different in old French.
2. Tell Blondel's story in his own words.
3. When an important person dies today the newspapers print an obituary – a story of their life which also tries to weigh up the good and bad things they did. Try to read one of these (you will find some in *The Times*) and then write obituaries for Richard and Saladin.

8 The later crusades

The Fourth Crusade

This was not the end of the crusades. In 1199 Pope Innocent III asked Christians to unite once again and journey to the eastern Mediterranean to help those who were still struggling against the Muslims. This time it was the barons of Europe and not the kings who responded to his preaching. Men came from Flanders (in the modern Netherlands), from France and from northern Italy and accepted the leadership of Boniface of Montferrat.

They met in Venice and decided to go to Egypt and defeat the Arabs in the heart of their empire, and then they hoped they could live more safely in the Holy Land. They made an agreement with the Venetians to give them ships, more soldiers, weapons and food. The Venetians asked £56,666, in return for supplying the crusaders with 4,500 knights and horses, 9,000 squires or young men to accompany them, and 20,000 foot soldiers. The Venetians also promised to give food for one year, but they said they wanted half of everything the crusaders won.

Geoffrey of Villehardouin

We know all these things about the Fourth Crusade because we have a book called *The Conquest of Constantinople* by Geoffrey of Villehardouin who was one of the men who went on the journey. He explains how the crusaders were unable to pay the Venetians all the money they asked, so they had to agree to help the Venetians in their own private war against the King of Hungary by taking the city of Zara on the Dalmatian Coast (in modern Yugoslavia).

The crusaders attacking Constantinople. This picture was drawn in the fourteenth century.

Even after this the crusaders did not stick to their plan to go to Egypt, but went to the city of Constantinople where they joined in a quarrel between two rivals who both wanted to rule the Byzantine empire. The ships of the crusaders and the Venetians sailed up the Golden Horn and landed easily because the Byzantines did not think they had come as enemies. Quarrels broke out between the greedy crusaders and the rich citizens of Constantinople.

Villehardouin describes what happened. The crusaders turned on the Byzantines and attacked them, finally setting fire to the houses.

> The army gained much **booty**; so much, indeed that no one could guess its amount or its value. It included gold and silver, table-services and precious stones, satin and silk, mantles of squirrel fur, ermine and **miniver**, and every choicest thing to be found on this earth.

Geoffrey of Villehardouin declared that, to his knowledge, so much booty had never been gained in any city since the creation of the world.

The crusaders then divided the Byzantine empire among themselves. Baldwin of Flanders became the first Frankish emperor and the Venetians took an enormous share, including part of the city of Constantinople, much of mainland Greece and many of the Greek islands. The Byzantine emperors remained in exile until 1261 when they won back Constantinople.

The Children's Crusade

Pope Innocent III was upset at the behaviour of the crusaders in the Fourth Crusade. Many people in western Europe lost their belief in the crusading idea, but in 1212 a group of children led by a shepherd boy called Stephen marched through France to Marseilles. They expected that God would divide the sea so that they could walk dry-footed to the Holy Land. They were very disappointed when this did not happen and some of the children returned home. The rest were offered free transport on ships by two merchants, Hugh the Iron and William the Pig. These bad men sold the children into slavery. This was the sad end of the Children's Crusade.

The last crusades

Other crusades were led by kings and nobles. In 1228 the emperor Frederick II went to the east, but he preferred to make peace with the Sultan al-Kamil of Egypt.

Sadly neither the Christians nor the Muslims liked promises made to their old enemies and the fighting went on. In 1249 the French king, who was to become St Louis because of his great holiness, went to Damietta in Egypt on crusade. He was then taken prisoner and had to pay a large sum of money to be released. More than twenty years later he went on crusade again, this time to fight against the Muslims in North Africa. The crusaders landed at Carthage near Tunis and made their camp. Plague broke out among the army of crusaders and the king himself died.

A fourteenth-century drawing of the capture of Damietta.

The Ottoman Turks capture Constantinople

In the fourteenth century a new and more powerful Muslim enemy arose, the Ottoman Turks. They gradually built up their empire in Asia Minor until in 1453 they were able to capture Constantinople and to destroy the Byzantine kingdom completely. In 1517 they overran the Arab lands of Egypt and seven years later they drove the Hospitallers from Rhodes. This empire, founded by the Ottomans, lasted until the twentieth century.

Things to do

1. Why was Pope Innocent III upset at what happened in the Fourth Crusade?
2. Write a story about one of the children who went on the Children's Crusade.
3. Find out if there are any crusader tombs or brass plates in a church near you. Draw the figures or learn how to rub the brasses.

How do we know?

We are lucky that a number of people living at the time wrote their accounts of the crusades. We can read descriptions of the crusades from the western and the Muslim points of view.

The Arabs were interested in writing history and they usually tried to be very fair about the events and people they described, pointing out the faults of the Arabs as well as their virtues. There are several accounts of Saladin's reign. One was written by his secretary, Imad ad-Din. He writes in a flowery style, but he tries to give a true picture of the Third Crusade, and he does not mind criticising his master. Another life of Saladin was written by his close friend, Baha ad-Din. Both these people knew the Sultan personally, so their books are very valuable.

One of the crusaders in the First Crusade, whose name we do not know, wrote about the terrible march across Asia Minor to Jerusalem. Archbishop William of Tyre also wrote *A History of the Things Which Happened Beyond the Seas*. This is a long book and he describes the people and battles in great detail. It was written first in Latin but was so popular that it was translated into French, which the nobles could read.

The journey of the Pilgrims and the deeds of King Richard is an account of the Third Crusade. It was probably written by a Templar, a religious knight, who wrote his book while the events were still 'warm' in his mind.

As well as written accounts of the crusades, we can also see the remains of the crusaders' castles in the Middle East. It is also possible to see the Citadel in Cairo with inscriptions of Saladin's time in it.

In museums you can see coins and armour from the time of the crusaders. Some churches have brass plates with crusaders on them. The Temple church in London even has **effigies** of

Templar knights. In the illustration below you can see that one of the knights has his legs crossed which, some say, shows that he died on crusade. You may be able to find a crusader brass in a church near you.

Effigies at the Temple church in London.

Things to do in a group

1. Invent a board game of one of the crusader journeys to the east. You could have some chance cards, for example 'Your ship is sinking and you must throw your armour overboard' or 'You are captured and must pay a ransom'.
2. Make a large picture of the siege of Acre, showing the town, the Christians besieging it and Saladin's army beyond. Include all the machines of war.
3. Why do you think the crusading idea came to such a bad end? Hold a class discussion about this. You could also think about the wars between people of different religions going on in the Middle East today. Are we any better than the crusaders were?

Glossary

adorn decorate
battering ram large wooden beam with a head of iron (for example, in the shape of a ram's head) used to beat down walls
bedouin Arabic tribes from Arabian, Syrian or North African deserts who lived a wandering life
booty treasure seized in war
breast-plate armour to protect the upper part of the body
chronicler person who makes a record of events (a **chronicle**)
cymbals musical instrument
dinar Arab gold coin
ducat western gold coin
effigy model of a person, usually in metal or stone
Frank westerner
hostage a prisoner who might be harmed if his friends did not do as they were told
idol image of God
Imam Muslim religious leader and teacher
infidel someone who does not believe in the same religious faith as you do
Koran the holy book of the Muslims
Kurds a people who live in Syria
Levant eastern end of the Mediterranean
massacre a killing of many people
minaret tower on a mosque
miniver white fur
minstrel singer or entertainer
mosque Muslim holy building
muezzin man who calls Muslims to prayer
Muslims followers of the religion of Islam, founded by Muhammad
obligation something that must be done
orb round ball
pilgrimage journey to a holy place
pilgrim person who went to visit holy places

scabbard case for a sword
scripture something written, usually a holy book
siege engines high platforms with machines for attacking walls
sheriffdom the job of a sheriff, one of the king's servants
solidus (plural **solidi**) western silver coin
supple bending easily
truce peace made between enemies for a short time

The names Levant, Holy Land or Syria meant in the Middle Ages the whole area now comprising Syria, Lebanon and Israel.

Index